C. Joseph Simmonts

ISBN: 87191-216-3
Library of Congress Catalog Card Number: 72-85040

61241-G

# GIANT CONDOR
## OF
## CALIFORNIA

*JULIAN MAY*

*Illustrations by Edwin Lee Huff*

**Creative Educational Society, Inc., Mankato, Minnesota 56001**

A huge bird circled slowly in the blue sky. His wings, black marked with white on the under side, spread nine feet from tip to tip. Of all the land birds in North America, he was the largest—a California condor.

Rising currents of air, warmed by the spring sun, helped hold him aloft. He glided around and around without flapping his wings for more than an hour. As he soared, his keen red eyes searched the ground for food. The condor was a scavenger, a member of the vulture family. His role in nature was the disposal of dead creatures.

A thousand feet below, a rancher paused in his work and looked up. The soaring condor was a majestic sight. The man knew it did useful work, too. When the rancher was a young boy, many more condors had circled over the valley. Now he was an old man—and there were only about forty condors left in all of North America.

The condor circled down the valley, coming lower so that he could watch the ground more easily. He passed over a dirt road, and there he saw the body of a jackrabbit that had been killed by a jeep the night before. Five turkey vultures, smaller relatives of the great condors, were gathered around it to feed.

The condor dropped down in a steep spiral. Feet extended, he landed near the carcass and walked toward it. The turkey vultures knew who was master. They hissed a bit, then stepped back to let the condor feed. When one young vulture tried to come forward, the condor flapped his great wings and hissed. The frightened young vulture stumbled back to wait its turn.

The condor nibbled rapidly with his large beak, holding the food animal with his feet. His feet were weak, not able to grasp prey. His head was bright orange, his upper neck gray. There were no feathers on either. A fluffy ruff of black feathers encircled his lower neck. Below that was an oval patch of bare skin, colored purplish red. This patch swelled up as the bird filled his crop with food.

When the condor was almost finished, a shadow passed over him. He looked up quickly—but it was too late. A golden eagle came diving down at him, seeking its share of the meat. The eagle struck the condor a glancing blow on the back. A few black feathers flew. It was time for the great bird to leave, since another, more masterful than himself, had arrived. The condor flapped slowly away. The eagle landed and started to eat. The poor vultures settled down to wait again—but all the eagle left them was the bones.

The condor soared away over the valley to the mountains on the other side. He went to a pool formed in the rock by a tiny stream. After scraping his beak on the ground to clean it, he bathed. Sparkling drops of water flew as he shook himself. He preened his feathers carefully until they were smooth, then spread his wings out in the sun to dry them.

He launched himself into the air again and flew deep into the mountains, to a cliff in an area far from roads. On the side of the cliff was a small cave. Inside the cave his mate was waiting, warming the egg. The male condor approached the nest warily and perched on a dead pine nearby. He looked about, but saw no enemies. It was safe to enter the cave.

There was no nest. The female rose up from the bare floor of the little cave to reveal a pale green egg about 4½ inches long. She had laid it 41 days before, and both parents had shared the work of brooding it. As the female condor flew away to eat and drink, the male settled down over the egg, tucking it under his great wing. His head drooped down, his eyes closed, and he slept.

Early in the afternoon, something woke him. He rose up on his legs and looked at the egg. It had cracked. The father bird stood looking down at it as the egg slowly opened. A pink little beak peeped out. Pieces of eggshell fell away. The chick lay on the ground—white, wet, and quite helpless. It shivered until its father's warm feathers covered it.

By the time the female returned to the cave, the chick was dry and fluffy. She was excited to see it and turned it gently with her beak to make sure that it was well. It was a female chick. Both parents looked at it for awhile. Then the mother settled over the baby while the male flew off to feed.

In the days that followed, both parents continued to warm the chick. And both fed her by opening their mouths wide and bringing up food for the little one to eat. The baby bird put her head right into the parents' mouths. Sometimes it seemed that they would swallow her, so eagerly did she rush after her food. She grew very quickly.

After six weeks, gray down had replaced the white fluff she was born with. Her parents now had to warm her only at night. But they fed her all through the summer. She grew larger and larger. Her feathers started to come in. By the end of September, she was fully feathered and ready to come out of the nest-cave and sit on the ledge nearby.

The young condor was now nearly as large as her parents. By herself, she learned to fly one day when the wind was strong enough to lift her great wings. But she went only a short way, landing on a tree growing out of the cliff.

All through the autumn and all through the storms of winter the parent birds continued to feed her. Her wings became stronger and stronger. But she was not able to search for her own food until spring. Then, full grown but still without the white adult feathers and orange-colored head, she was ready to fend for herself. The parents who had tended her so carefully would have a year's rest, then raise another chick.

The young female condor roosted at night in the secluded mountains, a wildlife refuge where she was safe from man. During the day, she searched for food over nearby ranches and forest land. It took her five years to become fully adult. Sometimes she spent her time with other young condors. Once, as she flew with a young male, she heard the sound of shooting.

The bird flying near her staggered in midair, then fell. The bullet of a hunter had taken his life. She did not understand what had happened to her companion. But from that time on, the sound of shots frightened her and sent her soaring quickly away.

One winter, the female condor flew over a valley ranch. She saw the body of a calf and alighted to feed on it. Nearby was a dead coyote. The female condor did not know that the rancher had poisoned the meat in order to kill coyotes that had been raiding his stock.

The female condor ate some of the meat. She became sick almost at once and could not fly. She hardly heard the sound of a jeep's motor. Her beautiful wings dragged on the ground and her head hung low as two men got out of the jeep and came close to her. They knew what had happened and they were sorry. They wanted to save the rare bird's life.

The men hurried off to get help. She became weaker and weaker. Within a short time, the condor warden from the Audubon Society came, wrapped her in sacking, and drove her to the zoo in a large city nearby.

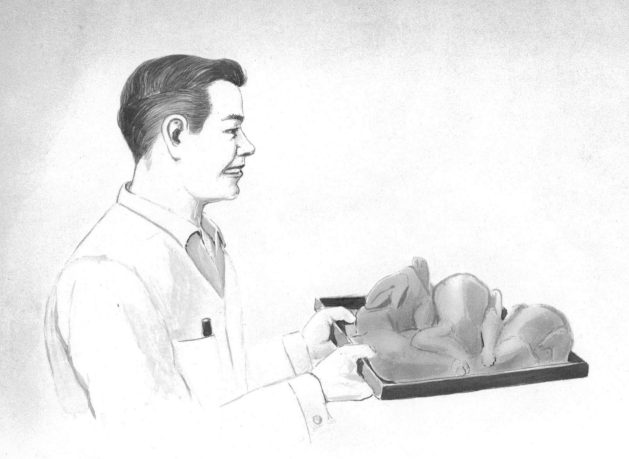

There a doctor began to treat her for poisoning. She was very frightened. But she was a gentle bird by nature and lay quietly as her human friends tried to help her.

The next day, the condor seemed much better. The medicine seemed to be working. She fed on some chicken and tried to stand up in the cage where she was resting. The doctor smiled at her. He felt sure she would get better soon—and he was right. Many visitors came to see her during the next week. She became bright-eyed and lively again.

C. Joseph Giumento

A few of the visitors thought she was an ugly bird. But those who had seen a condor in flight knew that she had a special kind of beauty. The early Indians had known that condors were remarkable. They had called the birds "bringers of thunder."

At last, when the doctor was certain that she was well, the young condor was taken home. The condor warden drove her to the refuge and set her free. She flew only a short distance, landing in a nearby tree.

She felt dizzy for a moment, but the feeling soon passed. She looked at the man who had helped her, and he waved at her. Strong winter winds whistled through the tree branches and through the feathers of her outspread wings. She launched herself from the tree and took off into the sky.

Higher and higher she went, circling the warden and his truck. Then finally she turned and headed for her roost in the mountains. The man watched her until she disappeared in the shining sky.

## ABOUT CALIFORNIA CONDORS

The condor has a wingspread of 8 to 9 feet and weighs from 20 to 30 pounds when full-grown. Both sexes look alike. Their bare heads and necks, which some people consider ugly, are really ideal for the birds' way of life. The skin is more easily cleaned than feathers after the bird has eaten. When cold weather arrives, the condor draws its bare head down into its fluffy ruff to keep warm.

California condors are closely related to the Andean condors of South America. Once the California species ranged all along the Pacific Coast of North America and eastward to Texas; but they were never very common. They reproduce slowly, laying a single egg only every two years. Young birds do not mate until they are five or six years old. If people come near the nesting site, the parents may abandon the egg. Condors can apparently abide the presence of man except during nesting time. Their two nesting areas in California—Sisquoc and Sespe Condor Sanctuaries—are closed to the public. The birds can be seen soaring over the Los Padres National Forest and nearby areas in southern California.

Condors have been on the verge of extinction for nearly 70 years. At first it was the fad of egg-collecting that endangered them. Then it was careless hunting and poison baits intended for other animals. This book is based on a true incident in which a poisoned condor was successfully nursed back to health. Now laws have been enacted to restrict the use of poison baits. The main danger that remains is man and his gun. If the giant condor is to be saved, people must learn that the idle shooting of large birds is not "fun." Only education can teach people that it is more enjoyable to watch a condor soaring in flight than it is to shoot the great bird dead.

C. Joseph Piummento